# Physician Assistants

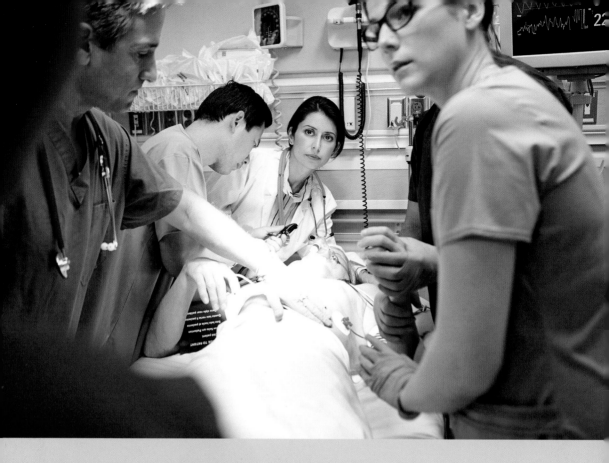

# Careers in Healthcare

**Athletic Trainers**
**Clinical & Medical Laboratory Scientists**
**Dental Hygienists**
**Dietitian Nutritionists**
**EMTs & Paramedics**
**Nurses**
**Occupational Therapists**
**Orthotists & Prosthetists**
**Physical Therapists**
**Physician Assistants**
**Respiratory Therapists**
**Speech Pathologists & Audiologists**
**Ultrasound Technicians**

CAREERS IN
HEALTHCARE

# Physician Assistants

Samantha Simon

MASON CREST
PHILADELPHIA

**Mason Crest**
450 Parkway Drive, Suite D
Broomall, PA 19008
www.masoncrest.com

Printed and bound in the United States of America.

CPSIA Compliance Information: Batch #CHC2017.
For further information, contact Mason Crest at 1-866-MCP-Book.

First printing
1 3 5 7 9 8 6 4 2

Library of Congress Cataloging-in-Publication Data

on file at the Library of Congress
ISBN: 978-1-4222-3804-2 (hc)
ISBN: 978-1-4222-7992-2 (ebook)

Careers in Healthcare series ISBN: 978-1-4222-3794-6

## QR CODES AND LINKS TO THIRD-PARTY CONTENT

# Table of Contents

## KEY ICONS TO LOOK FOR:

**Words to understand:** These words with their easy-to-understand definitions will increase the reader's understanding of the text while building vocabulary skills.

**Sidebars:** This boxed material within the main text allows readers to build knowledge, gain insights, explore possibilities, and broaden their perspectives by weaving together additional information to provide realistic and holistic perspectives.

**Educational Videos:** Readers can view videos by scanning our QR codes, providing them with additional educational content to supplement the text. Examples include news coverage, moments in history, speeches, iconic sports moments and much more!

**Text-dependent questions:** These questions send the reader back to the text for more careful attention to the evidence presented there.

**Research projects:** Readers are pointed toward areas of further inquiry connected to each chapter. Suggestions are provided for projects that encourage deeper research and analysis.

**Series glossary of key terms:** This back-of-the book glossary contains terminology used throughout this series. Words found here increase the reader's ability to read and comprehend higher-level books and articles in this field.

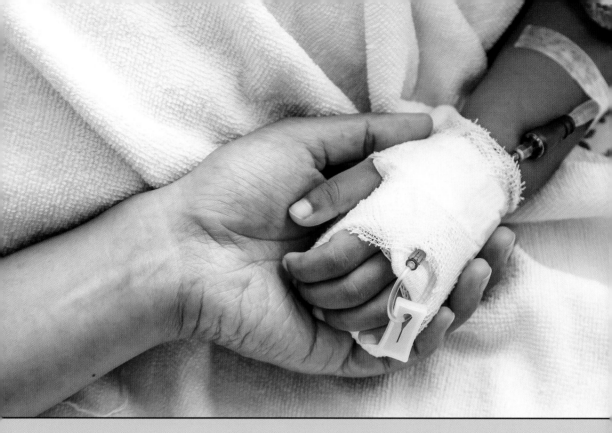

*Physician assistants see patients of all ages, and treat those with the most minor to the most severe diseases.*

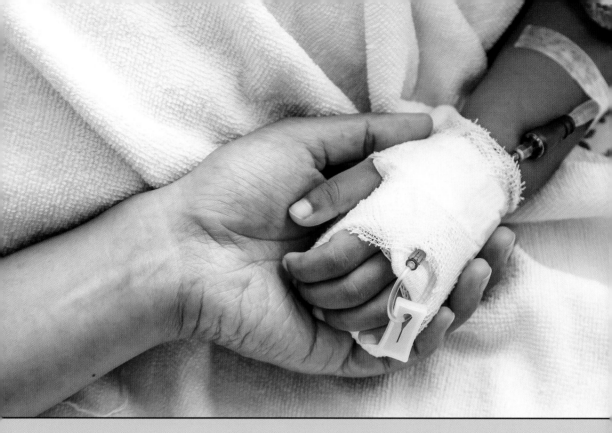 **Words to Understand in This Chapter**

**Affordable Care Act**—also known as Obamacare; a federal statute, passed in 2010, that allows greater access to affordable and quality health insurance for all US citizens.

**PAs**—physician assistants.

**physical assessment**—assessing the health status of patients by examining their physical symptoms and vitals.

**physician-PA teams**—collaborative health care teams made up of physicians and physician assistants.

**preventive medicine**—medicine and medical techniques designed to prevent any disease or disease symptoms. Examples include diet and exercise or even preventive medications.

# What Do Physician Assistants Do?

**A**s the health care system has changed substantially over the past few years, physician assistants have played a major role in how health care is adminis-tered. Physician assistants (*PAs*) help patients regain their health and well-being in times of sickness and help them con-tinue to lead healthy lives after treatment. PAs are both nation-ally and state certified, and they practice medicine on a team with physicians, surgeons, and other health care professionals. They are allowed to prescribe medication, perform certain pro-cedures, assist in surgeries, assess patients, and read laborato-ry results.

Physician assistants work hand in hand with doctors, nurs-es, and other health care personnel to ensure the best health care for their patients. *Physician-PA teams* follow a collaborative health care approach, which has been shown to improve health care outcomes and to promote *preventive medicine.* The US health care system is catching up to the collaborative model used in other countries, and has been reaping the benefits of team-based care. PAs can decrease demand for care through preventive approaches, education, and treatment. They allow physicians to see more patients during the business day by alleviating some of the routine work for physicians—such as doing *physical assessments* of patients, taking medical histories, or even assisting in the diagnosis of patient illness. With this type of teamwork, both physicians and physician assistants can treat more patients effectively in less time. As preventive care takes center stage in the US health care system, PAs are able to cut down on the population's overall health care needs, curb spending on health care, and lower the risk of disease among patients.

## The Value of Physician Assistants

With a general medicine education, PAs bring to their work a broad array of knowledge in multiple types of medicine. This allows PAs to choose one specialty and then move on to another, if they want. PAs can be found assisting in an operating room or assessing a patient in a primary care physician's office. With the shortage of medical professionals readily available to meet the ever-growing demands for health care services, PAs fill in gaps in the health care system so patients everywhere can receive quality care.

 **Did You Know?**

In its 2016 ranking of the best health care jobs in the United States, U.S. News and World Report ranked physician assistant fourth overall.

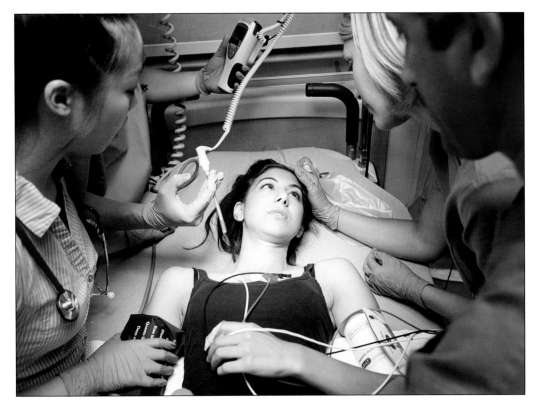

*Physicians and physician assistants work together to treat a patient.*

With the passing of the *Affordable Care Act* in 2010, health care in the United States has shifted its emphasis to providing health care for all Americans, while trying to reduce health care costs overall. The Affordable Care Act also enabled millions more people to obtain health insurance, increasing the demand for health care services. PAs figure prominently in contemporary health care under this reform by providing preventive care, enabling patients to spend more time with a health care professional, and offering more education for patients on how to stay healthy.

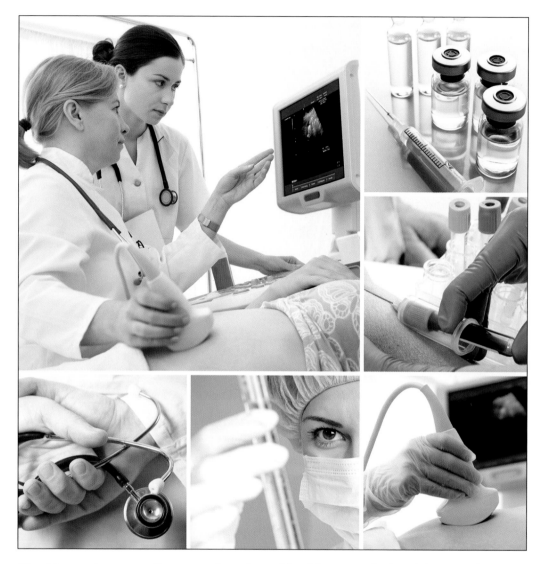

*Physician assistants are known as the universal healthcare professional, because they often have a broad array of general medical training.*

PAs take a holistic approach to health care, which dovetails with the contemporary direction in health care in the United States. They encourage constant communication with their

A physical therapist recounted the following story about an experience she had with a patient that will stay with her forever:

"Working in pediatric surgery, I work hand in hand with the hematology and oncology department because we put in all the metaports. These are the little buttons that go under the skin and are attached to a tube that connects to a major vein. They're designed so we can deliver medication to patients without having to stick them every time. This device is especially good for our long-term chemotherapy patients. So it is always a happy day when the hematology department asks us to remove a port, which means the kid is done with treatment and is ready to be discharged. Just last week we were asked to come in to remove a port from a little boy who had a very rare and highly malignant brain tumor. He had an almost zero percent chance to survive, but he beat it. It was just amazing to see, and to see that modern medicine really works. It was just incredible."

patients, and promote the same kind of communication among medical professionals, all with an eye toward coordinating care so they can make and keep their patients well. PAs look at each patient's overall medical condition, medical history, and whether the patient is being treated for an acute disease or a chronic condition. In working with their patients, they make

*As part of the health care team, physician assistants tend to spend more hands-on time with patients than physicians do.*

sure each one understands his treatment plan, how to prevent his disease from progressing any further, and how he should be responding to treatment.

Physician assistants spend more hands-on time with patients than physicians do, both before and during exams and diagnosis. This gives physicians more time to accurately and efficiently diagnose and support patients, reducing health care costs in many ways. The more time the patient spends with a PA, the more time the patient gets for proper patient education and discussion about her concerns or questions regarding treatment or any other issues related to her health. The more educated and knowledgeable a patient becomes about her medical

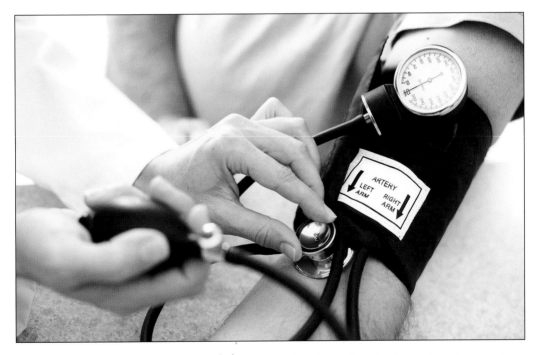

*High blood pressure can be successfully mitigated if the patient is educated and treated correctly. Physician assistants help in the prevention and education of many diseases like high blood pressure.*

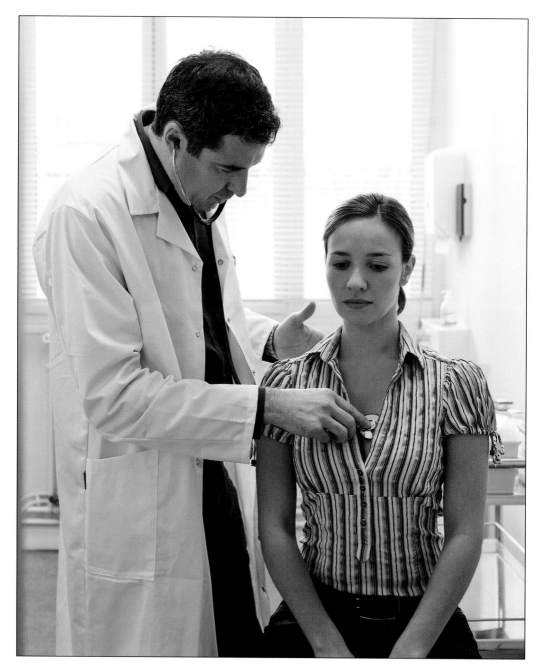

*PAs are expected to alleviate some of the routine work for physicians, such as performing physical assessments of patients and taking medical histories.*

treatments and conditions, the fewer return doctor visits she needs to make, the fewer instances of wrongful medication administration there are, and the greater her understanding of how to properly monitor her medical conditions. This kind of education also leads to fewer hospital admissions and readmissions, and more preventive health care on the part of patients and patients' families and loved ones.

## Educational Video

For a short video that shows what a PA does, scan here:

## Text-Dependent Questions

1. How do PAs promote preventive medicine?
2. What does PA stand for?
3. Are PAs just state certified? Or are they also nationally certified?

## Research Project

The next time you go to your doctor's office, ask if a physician assistant works there. If so, ask the PA how he or she works collaboratively with the physician and how he or she uses a teamwork approach to take care of patients.

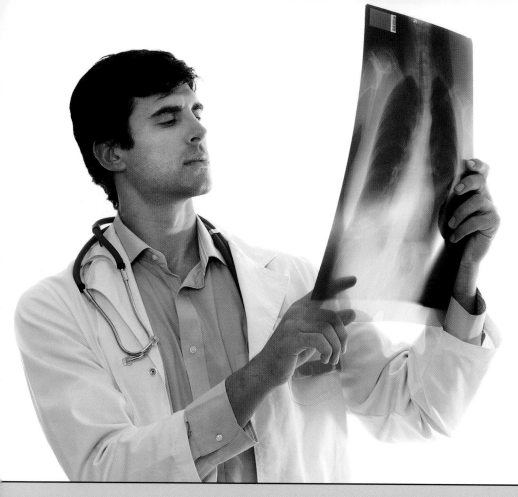

*Physician assistants are taught how to utilize X-rays when diagnosing patients.*

## Words to Understand in This Chapter

**CT scan**—computerized tomography scan; this type of radiological imaging test uses various x-ray images to create images of bones, blood vessels, and soft tissues.

**dermatology**—the study of the skin.

**radiology**—the study of diagnostic imaging.

**subspecializing**—learning more about a specific specialty; for example, a PA specializing in surgery might then subspecialize in orthopedic surgery.

**trauma bays**—sections of the emergency rooms designated specifically for the treatment of major trauma patients.

# A Look at the Opportunities

In most medical professions, you can choose to specialize. This is true for physician assistants as well. Before specializing, a physician assistant must become a licensed physician assistant by going through a rigorous physician assistant master's program, which takes between two and two and half years to complete. After they receive their license, physician assistants can opt to specialize, much as physicians do. If a PA decides to specialize, he must go through specialty programs that include over a thousand clinical hours and further education. The specialties range from gynecology to *dermatology*. Here are the top-paying specialties for physician assistants.

## Radiology

*Radiology* is the study of diagnostic imaging. Diagnostic imag-

*Urgent care is one of the most popular specialties for physician assistants in the United States. Many physician assistants do their training rotations in urgent care facilities.*

ing can range from ultrasounds to *CT scans*. Radiology specialties are very high paying. If a PA specializes in radiology, she would be working under the supervision of a radiologist and could perform fluoroscopies, interpret scans or x-rays, do nee-

**Did You Know?**

The US Department of Labor's Bureau of Labor Statistics projects a 30 percent growth rate for physician assistants through 2024.

dle biopsies, and insert and remove IV catheters. Radiology is a growing field. The average patient may undergo up to two radiological exams during a regular doctor visit. The average salary for radiology PAs is around $150,000 per year.

## Urgent Care

Another of the highest-paid specialties in the physician assistant field is urgent care. PAs in this field earn a median annual salary of around $130,000. This salary can go up to $150,000 or more, depending on the region where the PA works. Urgent care PAs treat patients with an array of different ailments. These PAs also get to work more regular hours than other PAs, but can still work weekends and nights, if they choose to.

Urgent care clinics usually provide care for injuries that are not as serious as those seen in emergency rooms. These may range from broken bones to ear infections and everything in between. The variety of illnesses and injuries, together with the set work hours, make urgent care clinics appealing work environments for PAs.

# Emergency Medicine

This specialty attracts adrenaline junkies. Working in the emergency room is a constant rush. Shifts for emergency room physician assistants usually average between ten and twelve hours, and the illnesses and injuries they treat are exceedingly varied. Some of the procedures that PAs perform as an ER physician assistant are suturing lacerations, collecting medical histories, assisting with diagnoses, making incisions and draining abscesses, performing lumbar punctures, and applying casts and splints. This is one of the most common specialties for physician assistants. In this specialty a physician assistant works under an emergency room doctor in the fast-paced ER environment. Emergency room physician assistants can treat a range of patients, from those requiring acute care to those in the major *trauma bays*. The average salary of an emergency medicine physician assistant is around $115,000 a year.

# Surgical Specialties

Just as it is for physicians, surgery is a very high-paying specialty for PAs. It is also one of the most difficult and strenuous physician assistant specialties. PAs who specialize in surgery often work night shifts, are constantly on call, and are on their feet throughout each surgical procedure they assist with. After becoming a certified physician assistant, the PA must then enter a surgical residency program specifically for physician assistants. Some of these residency programs focus on a particular type of surgery. For example, a PA may take a residency in thoracic or orthopedic surgery. This is very similar to the residency programs that physicians go through after medical

*Hospital emergency rooms (ERs) currently employ more physician assistants than they do ER physicians.*

*Physician assistants who specialize in dermatology are able to perform exams that screen for various skin diseases.*

*Physician assistants are able to perform certain procedures and help with surgeries.*

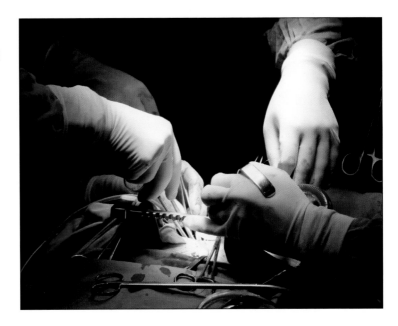

school. Surgical PAs may specialize even further by *subspecializing*. Their salary usually begins at upwards of $113,000, depending on the surgical specialty and the number of years of experience they have. Surgical PAs work under a supervising surgeon and can suture lacerations, do surgical assisting, offer post-operative and pre-operative care, and conduct diagnostic testing.

## Dermatology

Dermatology is the study of the skin. Dermatology physician assistants work under a dermatologist in the care and management of proper skin care. This is one of the most lucrative specialties for physician assistants and physicians alike. This specialty is very appealing to medical professionals because the hours are generally regular, emergencies are infrequent, and

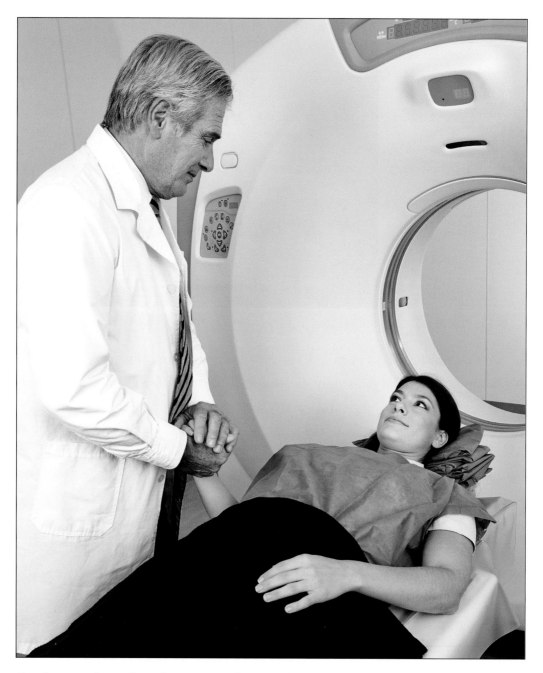

*Oncology, or the study and treatment of cancerous tumors, is a growing field for physician assistants.*

the salaries are high. The procedures that dermatology PAs can perform include excisions, skin biopsies, laser therapies, and Botox injections. The average salary for a dermatology physician assistant is around $113,000 a year, which is almost $40,000 more per year than a non-specialized physician assistant. This salary can go as high as $130,000 a year because of the amount of cosmetic dermatology done in the office.

### Educational Video

Scan here to learn what it takes to be a dermatology physician assistant:

## Text-Dependent Questions

1. What are some of the procedures that dermatology physician assistants can perform?
2. What is radiology?
3. Surgical physician assistants must complete what type of program after graduating from physician assistant school?

## Research Project

Look up some out-of-the-ordinary physician assistant specialties not mentioned in this chapter. Then research if there are any local PAs with those specialties in your area.

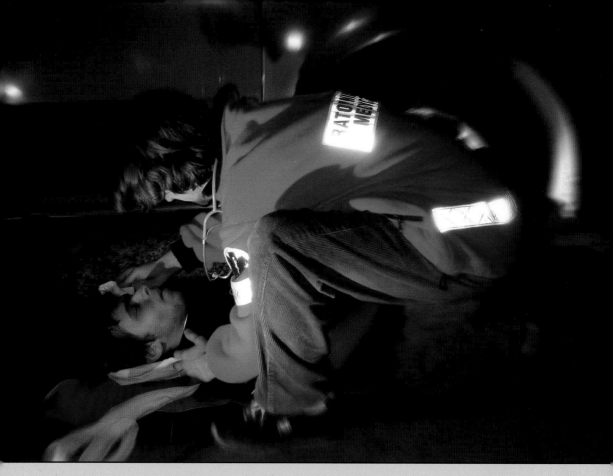

*Many physician assistant programs require an interested person to get field experience before they can apply to the program. Many aspiring PAs gain the experience they need by shadowing an EMT, or even becoming certified in this field.*

## 📖 Words to Understand in This Chapter

**clinical rotations**—shadowing of medical professionals in different fields and specialties as part of a PA's education. During clinical rotations aspiring professionals gain hands-on experience with patients under the supervision of an attending medical professional.

**EMT**—emergency medical technician; a specially trained medical professional who is certified to provide basic emergency services before and during transport to a hospital.

**NCCPA**—National Commission on Certification of Physician Assistants.

**PANCE**—Physician Assistant National Certifying Exam.

# Education and Training

**A** career as a physician assistant is one of the fastest-growing careers in the medical profession today. Employment of physician assistants is projected to grow 30 percent from 2014 to 2024. Among the reasons for this surge in the need for PAs are changes in the health care landscape, including the aging of the baby boomer population and the passage of the Affordable Care Act. Physician assistants are in great demand to fill gaps in providing health care. This career is highly sought-after because the hours you work are regular and you earn a good salary, but the road to becoming a PA is no easy task.

In high school, students who have decided to pursue this career are encouraged to take a large science course load, earn good SAT scores for college, and even become certified nursing

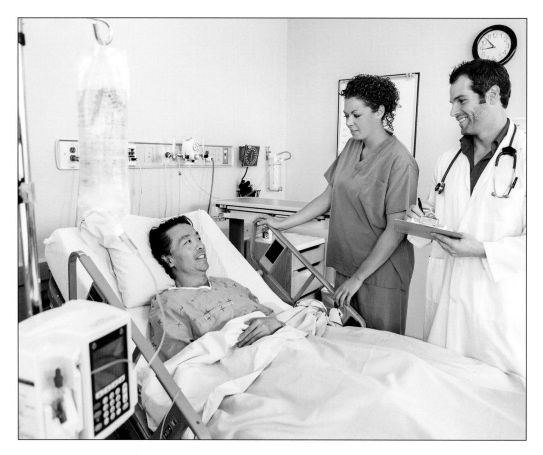

*In most cases, about half of a university's physician assistant coursework involves clinical rotations. This allows physician assistants to experience working in many different types of medical facilities.*

assistants after they complete their high school education. Undergraduate education is crucial for aspiring PAs. Most applicants to physician assistant schools have a bachelor's degree and some health care–related work experience. While admissions requirements vary from program to program, most programs require two to four years of undergraduate course-work with a focus on science. Undergraduates with non-science-related degrees can still apply to PA school, but must take at least two years of science classes, such as anatomy, biology, chemistry, and other health sciences. In addition to an undergraduate degree, most PA programs also require PA candidates to perform a minimum of a hundred hours working in a clinical setting. These

**Educational Video**

To hear a physician assistant talk about her educational experiences, scan here:

clinical hours can come from working as a medical scribe, a certified nursing assistant, an *EMT*, or any other clinical medical work.

In the United States there are about 200 different PA programs. From the moment a student decides that she wants to become a PA, she must start preparing to apply for PA schools. Undergraduate students applying to a PA school must have a competitive grade point average, a good work and educational resume, and an above-average graduate record examination (GRE) score. The requirements and minimum scores depend on the PA program and the school students are applying to. Another road to becoming a physician assistant includes completing a demanding physician assistant bachelor's degree (BA-PA). Very few schools offer the BA-PA degree program, which is very rigorous, but this allows students to receive a bachelor's degree while simultaneously earning a graduate-level PA certificate which is equivalent to a Masters Degree. This type of program is a way for students to save both time and money.

## In PA School

The length of the PA school program is usually 24 to 30 months, depending on the school and the program. When searching for a PA program, students must look for programs that are accredited by the Accreditation Review Commission on Education for the Physician Assistant (ARC-PA). When entering PA school, most physician assistant students can expect to receive an education in pathology, anatomy, clinical medical laboratory science, physiology, clinical medicine, pharmacology, medical ethics, and other clinical medicine courses. While completing their in-class education, PA students also

## A PA Talks About Her Training

A physician assistant who is currently working in the field was asked to describe the schooling and hands-on training that she needed to gain her current job. Specifically, she was asked how many years she spent in PA school, what types of classes she took, and what kinds of hands-on training she was required to complete in order to fulfill the requirements for her degree. Her response was as follows:

"I got a undergraduate degree in fine art and graphic design. I then went back and did my science prerequisites for PA school. I did not have any hands-on training, but PA schools do require you to do shadowing hours with a PA to figure out if becoming a PA is really for you. So I did do some shadowing hours."

*The twenty-four to thirty months of PA programs are known to be the most grueling time of a physician assistant's education*

gain hands-on training with thousands of hours in *clinical rotations*. These rotations range from specialties, like gynecology, to internal medicine. Much time is devoted to general medical education specialties, such as family medicine, emergency medicine, and pediatrics. There is a huge emphasis on primary care in ambulatory clinics, physicians' offices, and acute and long-term care facilities. These two years are known to be among the most grueling and difficult times of a PA's career. Upon graduation from PA school, students will earn a master's degree in physician assistant studies.

# Certification and Licensing

Once physician assistants graduate from PA school, they are required to be nationally licensed as well as licensed to practice in their own state. To become licensed nationally, PAs must pass the Physician Assistant National Certifying Examination (*PANCE*), administered by the National Commission on Certification of Physician Assistants (*NCCPA*). The test is five hours long and consists of 300 multiple-choice questions designed to assess basic medical and surgical knowledge. If students fail the exam the first time, they may take the test up to six times over a period of six years.

This licensing means that a PA can serve as a physician assistant in all 50 states, and all American territories. A physician assistant who passes the exam may use the credential Physician Assistant–Certified (PA-C). This is akin to physicians putting the acronym MD after their name. PAs then must take and pass a state exam to practice medicine in the state they choose to work in. In addition to obtaining both state and national licensing, PAs are required to renew their licensing and certifications every six to ten years. To get their licensing renewed, they must complete 100 hours of continuing education every two years as well. These requirements are a must for PAs to maintain their licensing nationally; there are different requirements at the state level and these vary from state to state.

*Physician assistants are constantly learning and re-educating themselves. To maintain their certification, physician assistants must take over two hundred hours of additional education courses every two years.*

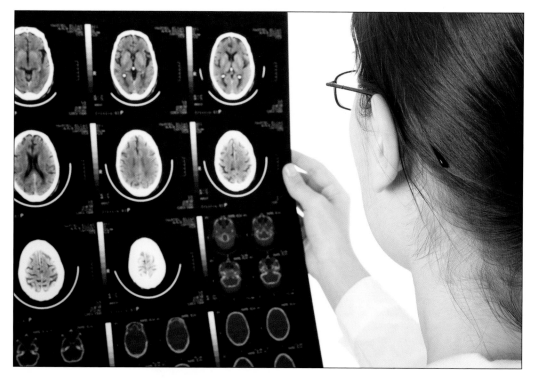

*Radiology is just one of the many subspecialties that Physician Assistants can choose from.*

## Further Education for Physician Assistants

Education does not stop at the master's level for PAs. Some physician assistants pursue additional education in a medical specialty. These programs are very similar to residency programs for physicians. Post-graduate educational programs are available in areas such as emergency medicine, surgery, and other specialties. To apply and qualify to enter one of these programs, a physician assistant must be a graduate of an accredited PA program and must have received a license from the NCCPA.

Another way for physician assistants to expand their knowledge and status is by applying for managerial positions. For example, an experienced physician assistant may supervise other staff and even become a professor once obtaining a doctorate degree which allows them to teach aspiring physician assistants. Some physician assistants also become executives in health care organizations or medical practices.

## Text-Dependent Questions

1. True or False: PAs have to be licensed both by the state where they practice and nationally.
2. What degree must a PA have before entering PA school?
3. How long is PA school?

## Research Project

Look up PA schools in your local area. Check how many are in your city, county, and state.

*Duke University was the first American college or university to operate a physician assistant program.*

## Words to Understand in This Chapter

**Certificate of Added Qualifications (CAQ) programs**—CAQ programs allow PAs to earn formal recognition of their specialized expertise in whatever specialty they choose to pursue.

**NBME**—National Board of Medical Examiners.

**PA program**—a physician assistant post-graduate educational program. This program is usually 24 months in length and includes both in-class instruction and clinical rotations.

# Evolution of Physician Assistants

**T**he first physician assistant program was founded in 1965 at Duke University in Durham, North Carolina, by Dr. Eugene Stead Jr. Recognizing the shortage of primary care physicians at that time, Dr. Stead set up a medical training program for four naval corpsmen who had experience in medicine from their military service. The program was designed to train medical professionals in a shorter amount of time than it took to train a medical doctor. Yet the program would give these professionals an understanding of the broader and more generalized medical curriculum required to assist an MD.

This original *PA program* was, in some ways, modeled after the relationship between Dr. Amos Johnson and his assistant Henry Lee "Buddy" Treadwell. At this time in medicine, pro-

*US Army doctors walk to their classes at the army's medical field service school in Carlisle, Pennsylvania, 1943. The education of physician assistants is based on fast-track training of doctors that was implemented during the Second World War.*

fessional relationships like this were very common. The relationship between Treadwell and Johnson began as Dr. Johnson utilizing Treadwell as an orderly, moving patients, changing sheets, and other demands around the clinic. With time, Dr. Johnson began to teach and let Treadwell observe in procedures, chemistry test, and even allowed him to take and develop x-ray films. Dr. Johnson was a very willing teacher and knew he needed assistance running his solo practice. The relationship eventually progressed over time to where Treadwell was referred to as Dr. Johnson's assistant and Dr. Johnson even felt comfortable leaving his practice with Treadwell when he was away. This relationship was the foundation to the Physician-Physician Assistant team. This ultimately led to the development of the Duke PA program. On October 6, 1967, three naval officers—Victor H. Germino, Kenneth F. Ferrell, and Richard J. Scheele—became the first graduates of the Duke University physician assistant program.

*The first class of the Duke University Physician Assistant Program was compromised of military corpsmen.*

In 1968, the American Academy of Physician Assistants was created, with the Duke PA graduates as the founding members. By the early 1970s, hundreds of physician assistant programs starting cropping up around the country, but each program varied in length and quality of instruction. This led to the development of a classification system for PA programs by the Board of Medicine of the National Academy of Sciences. The system classified each program as type A, type B, or type C. Type A programs were wide-ranging programs that were two years long and broadly trained students in many different medical specialties and primary care medicine. Type B programs trained assistants in a specific specialty. Type C programs,

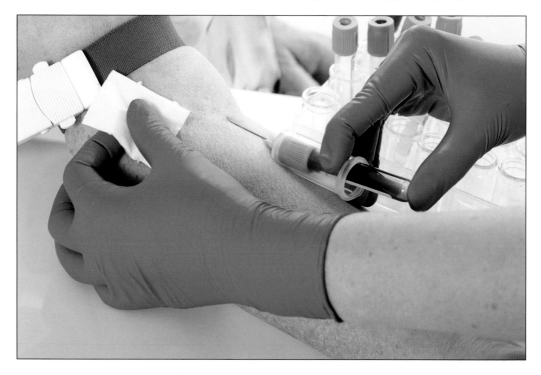

*Almost fifty-three percent of PAs practicing in this country today specialize in primary care medicine.*

meanwhile, trained future PAs in generalized medicine, but in a shorter period of time and with a less in-depth curriculum. From this classification, PA programs were required to become type A programs nationally.

**Educational Video**

Scan here for a brief video about the history of physician assistant programs:

In 1971 the four pillars of the physician assistant profession were established. They are (1) a society of practitioners, (2) an association of educational programs training those practitioners, (3) a nationally recognized body charged with accreditation of the programs, and (4) a process of certification of graduates in the public interest. These four pillars made PA programs more uniform nationally. After the profession of physician assistant was established, an additional national examination was created in 1973. The National Board of Medical Examiners (*NBME*) administered the first certifying examination for physician assistants to primary care physicians. This exam was given to 880 candidates; 10 percent of those taking the exam were graduates of nurse-practitioner programs and the rest were physician assistant graduates. A year later, the NCCPA was established in Atlanta. To formulate uniform standards for the physician assistant community, 14 national

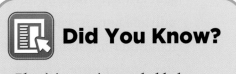

**Did You Know?**

Physician assistants held about 94,400 jobs in the most recent year for which data is available.

health care organizations came together in 1974 to form the National Commission on Certification of Physician Assistants (NCCPA). NCCPA was established to provide oversight regarding eligibility and standards for the NBME examination, and to assure state medical boards, employers, and the public of the competency of PAs. That year, Thomas E. Piemme, MD, was elected as the first president of the NCCPA, and David L. Glazer was selected as the first executive director. From that point on, the NCCPA was the governing body that established uniform standards and regulations for PA programs throughout the nation.

From 1974 to the present, PA programs, with the help of funds from the NCCPA and other federal funding, have grown in both number and quality of education. According to *Forbes* and *Money* magazines, the physician assistant master's degree has been one of the most desirable degrees in recent years, because of the passing of the Affordable Care Act, also known as Obamacare, in 2010. This act vastly expanded the number of people in the United States with health insurance coverage, and the need for PAs grew exponentially as a result. The Affordable Care Act spells out how essential PAs are to providing primary and preventive medicine in new health care programs and structures across the nation. Obamacare put in place policies and procedures more oriented toward preventive medicine, and maintaining health and well-being. These changes in the health care system are very similar to the pillars and philosophies of physician assistants. With 53 percent of the nation's practicing PAs specializing in primary care, PAs contribute substantially to the current health care system and will continue to do so as the need for primary care physicians grows.

In 2011, the National Commission on Certification of Physician Assistants (NCCPA) developed *Certificate of Added Qualifications (CAQ) programs*. These CAQ programs allow PAs to earn formal recognition of their specialized expertise, whether it is in cardiovascular and thoracic surgery, emergency medicine, nephrology, orthopedic surgery, or psychiatry. These CAQ programs and examinations allow PAs to expand their knowledge and qualifications. The first CAQ examination was given nationally on September 12, 2011. PAs have also begun

*Physician assistants work on health-care teams, along with nurses and physicians, to bring better-quality healthcare to their patients.*

## A PA Talks About Her Mentor

A physician assistant who is currently working in the field was asked to talk about a person that she looked up to in the profession, and why. She responded:

"When I was in PA school, I was doing my rotations. I did one of my elective rotations in the neonatal intensive-care unit. And I remember being amazed by this PA who had been working there 30 years. She was the go-to person for everything. She knew everything about everything. Everyone would come to her—doctors, nurses, the whole department would go to her for advice. I would love to be that person one day, and working in a department for that long and collecting all that knowledge. That is what I strive to be."

to transition to a new ten-year certification maintenance process. This ten-year certification includes new requirements for self-assessment and performance improvement and more educational training and professional growth. It runs on five two-year cycles that require submitting proof of 100 clinical hours worked in various subcategories, along with a certification fee at the end the required renewal year.

Physician assistants are also growing in their relationships with physicians and their practices. Physicians are taking on a larger number of physician assistants, especially in large primary care practices and practices that cater to more rural and underserved communities where practicing physicians, especially specialists, are few and far between. This career offers a high level of job satisfaction and is often ranked as one of the best medical professions to work in. Why? Because of the high pay and how much of a difference you can make in the health care system today. Many studies have shown that PAs add a lot of value to a medical practice. Their collaborative methods enable a practice to see patients faster, pay more attention to patients and their medical histories and needs, and perform more effective follow-up care.

 **Text-Dependent Questions**

1. Are physicians taking on a larger or smaller number of physician assistants?
2. Where was the first PA program developed?

**Research Project**

Look up the number-one ranked PA program in your state, in the nation, and in the world.

*Physician assistants are trained to use a variety of new technologies throughout their day at work, from diagnostic tools to databases that house medical records electronically.*

## 📖 Words to Understand in This Chapter

**medical providers**—professionals that help and execute medical care for the public.

**prescribe**—means to order prescriptions for patients.

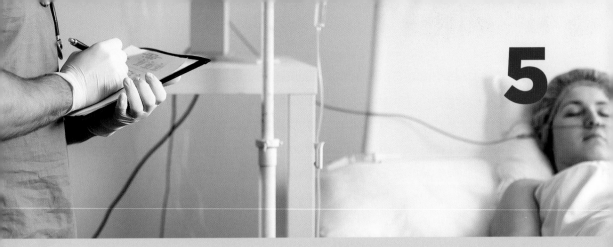

# Overview and Interview

F rom the time they first appeared on the health care scene, physician assistants have done nothing but help improve health care in the United States. The first physician assistant program was founded in 1965 at Duke University in Durham, North Carolina, by Dr. Eugene Stead Jr. in response to the shortage of physicians at the time. Since the passing of the Affordable Care Act in 2010, the shortage of medical professionals and the increase in the number of people who have health insurance coverage in the United States has placed PAs in high demand. PAs are filling this gap for medical professionals throughout the nation. PAs allow for medicine to be brought to places and patients in need, such as rural areas and highly populated areas.

To become a physician assistant, you must obtain a bachelor's degree, and then complete a rigorous physician assistant master's degree program. This program can be between two and two and a half years and consists of clinical rotations and classroom learning. After finishing this program, physician assistants take the Physician Assistant National Certifying Examination (PANCE) from the National Commission on Certification of Physician Assistants (NCCPA). This certification allows physician assistants to become nationally certified. PAs must also take a state certification exam, depending on which state they choose to practice in. After passing national and state certification exams, physician assistants can opt to specialize, just like physicians. They can specialize in surgery, dermatology, emergency medicine, or any other medical specialty. The training for PAs never stops. They must complete 100 hours of education after they are certified every two years and are required to be recertified every ten years.

Physician assistants and their physician teams provide health care to more and more patients throughout the day. According to the American Academy of Family Physicians and American Academy of Physician Assistants, these physician–physician assistant teams are serving more communities, with better and more efficient medical care. PAs have been instrumental in shaping health care in the United States and responding to patient needs, both in the past and looking ahead to the future.

# Q&A with a Professional in the Field

*Jenny Rizel*

What follows is an interview with Jenny Rizel, a physician assistant working in the field today.

**QUESTION: How long have you been a physician assistant?**

**Jenny:** "Two years."

**QUESTION: What was your inspiration to get into this field or work?**

**Jenny:** "Ever since I was a kid, I knew I wanted to do something in the field of science and medicine. When I was in the fourth grade, I actually wrote a book report about a book on orthopedic surgery. I was just fascinated by medicine and the human body, and I knew from that point I would want to pursue something in medicine and science. But when I was in college, I got my degree in fine art and graphic design and then went back to school later to complete my science prerequisites for PA school. I chose to become a PA because I loved the model. I love how PAs work in any field, anywhere, and a PA can earn her master's degree in two years. I was actually married with four kids at the time I decided to pursue a career in the medical field, and going to medical school and going through that process did not seem like the right model for me. The PA model worked really well with my lifestyle."

## Question: What is your specialty and why did you choose it?

**Jenny:** "I specialized in pediatric surgery. I love surgery, I love the operating room, and I love the atmosphere. Also, I wanted to work with children. I love children. I was actually a preschool teacher prior to going to PA school. I knew I always wanted to work with kids."

## QUESTION: What has been the most challenging aspect of your job?

**Jenny:** "I would say dealing with the loss of a patient—whether from trauma or cancer. It is very hard."

## QUESTION: What is the most rewarding?

**Jenny:** "To see a kid get better. That is amazing to me."

**QUESTION: What would you say to a young adult considering a career as a PA?**

**Jenny:** "I think it is a great option for people who want to practice medicine. The best part is that, as a PA, you can work in any medical setting. I think it is a great option for anyone. The schooling is hard—it is two-year degree at a master's level so it is an intense two years; you have to work really hard. Students have to realize going in that those two years are not easy. But once you are done, the career itself is very rewarding. So I would recommend it to anyone who wants to be in the medical field."

*The Affordable Care Act was signed into federal law by President Barack Obama on March 23, 2010. In its first seven years, studies indicated that the Act provided health insurance to 16.4 million people who did not previously have it.*

**QUESTION: To get your specialty in pediatric surgery, did you have to go to any residency program or any extended programs after PA school?**

**Jenny:** "No. PAs in pediatric surgery are not required to undergo any further training. There are residencies available for PAs who want to continue their education. But for pediatric surgery it is not required."

---

**QUESTION: What kind of personal traits do you think are important for a physician assistant to have?**

**Jenny:** "I think it is important for anybody in the medical field to be open-minded and to really listen to their patients and not just assume things. I think that is the biggest thing you can come away with and understand—that you don't just walk into a room and immediately think, 'Oh, this is the problem and I know how to fix it.' You have to listen to what the real problem is and what your patient is telling you and what the patient's issues are."

## Did You Know?

Physician assistants are *medical providers* who are licensed to diagnose and treat illness and disease. They can *prescribe* medication for patients, take medical histories, and even perform certain procedures. Physician assistants are found in physicians' offices, hospitals, and clinics. They work in collaboration with a licensed physician as a team, but can grow in education and specialty at any point.

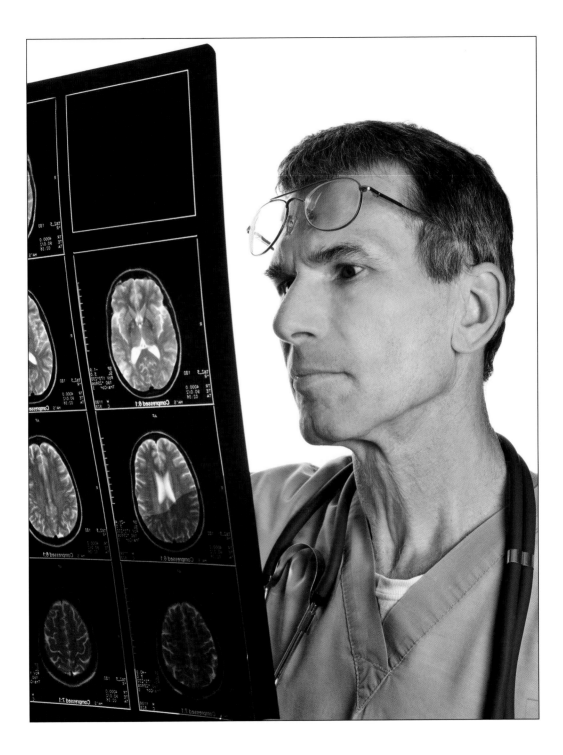

**QUESTION: Let's talk about the emotional side of being a PA. Have you experienced traumatic events in your profession in which you have had to separate yourself from the sadness (such as losing a patient or tending to a very sick child)? What kind of advice would you give new PAs on how to deal with this aspect of the job?**

**Jenny:** "That happens all the time. I work in trauma so, unfortunately, you see sad things in the trauma bay. That's part of the job and what happens in this field. It is just very sad. I always need time after something sad happens to sit and think about it and get over it. You never really get over it, but you have to realize that you have to disconnect—you can't take it home with you, especially when sad things happen to children. But you cannot let that affect you because then you cannot work the next day."

---

**QUESTION: PA shifts are much different from those in the corporate world. Can you please explain the kinds of shifts a PA is expected to work, and talk a little about the toll these can take on your body, mind, and overall health?**

**Jenny:** "That varies according to what setting you're in—an office, a clinic, or a hospital—and the type of practice you're in. I work three days a week, 13-hour shifts. That is full time, just more condensed. I like that I am off four days, but I know PAs who work five days a week, and work nine to five. I also know PAs who work seven days on, and seven days off. It just depends on your preference, what you like, and what setting you're in.

## QUESTION: Explain being on call. How does that work for PAs?

**Jenny:** "I'm never on call from home. We have someone in my department 24/7, 365. So because my shifts are set up that way, I work my entire shift and I am at the hospital the whole time. Some people are on call from home; some people are on call in-house and then go home. That is one of the reasons I like being a PA: There is such a broad range of how you work and what you practice.

## QUESTION: What kind of technology do you use each day?

**Jenny:** "All the health records are computerized, so I am on the computer all the time. There are a lot of apps for a lot of things. I used to use an app that would calculate drip rates and Hippocrates is also a great app I use to tell you the side effects of medications."

**Educational Video**

Scan here to hear a physical therapist talk about the pros and cons of the profession.

**QUESTION: Is this job what you expected when you first made the decision to get into this field?**

**Jenny:** "Yes."

---

**QUESTION: Are there certain specialties within the physician assistant profession that are most in demand today and therefore have the most job opportunities and job security?**

**Jenny:** "Primary care is the most needed at the moment."

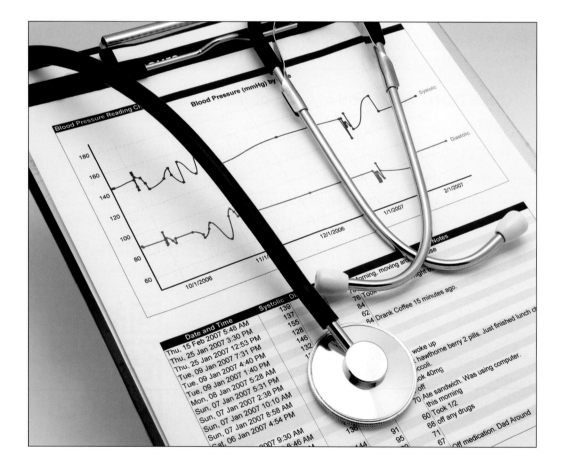

**QUESTION: What kind of income can a PA expect to make starting out? Similarly, what does an established physician assistant typically make?**

**Jenny:** "It varies by state and specialty. But it does go up by years of experience and specialty."

---

**QUESTION: In your mind, what makes for a successful PA?**

**Jenny:** "Someone who is willing to listen. Someone who listens to the team, the nurses, the supervising physician, and especially the patients. You have to be a team player because teamwork makes health care work."

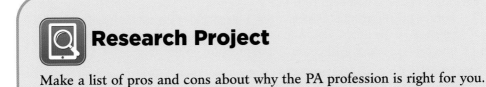

## Text-Dependent Questions

1. What type of technology do physician assistants use every day?
2. What are some very important traits for PAs to have?

## Research Project

Make a list of pros and cons about why the PA profession is right for you.

# Series Glossary

**accredited**—a college or university program that has met all of the requirements put forth by the national organization for that job. The official stamp of approval for a degree.

**Allied Health Professions**—a group of professionals who use scientific principles to evaluate, diagnose and treat a variety of diseases. They also promote overall wellness and disease prevention in support of a variety of health care settings. (These may include physical therapists, dental hygienists, athletic trainers, audiologists, etc.)

**American Medical Association (AMA)**—the AMA is a professional group of physicians that publishes research about different areas of medicine. The AMA also advocates for its members to define medical concepts, professions, and recommendations.

**anatomy**—the study of the structure of living things; a person and/or animal's body.

**associate's degree**—a degree that is awarded to a student who has completed two years of study at a junior college, college, or university.

**bachelor's degree**—a degree that is awarded to a student by a college or university, usually after four years of study.

**biology**—the life processes especially of an organism or group.

**chemistry**—a science that deals with the composition, structure, and properties of substances and with the transformations that they undergo.

**cardiology**—the study of the heart and its action and diseases.

**cardiopulmonary resuscitation (CPR)**—a procedure designed to restore normal breathing after cardiac arrest that includes the clearance of air passages to the lungs, mouth-to-mouth method of artificial respiration, and heart massage by the exertion of pressure on the chest.

**Centers for Disease Control**—the Centers for Disease Control and Prevention (CDC) is a federal agency that conducts and supports health promotion, prevention and preparedness activities in the United States with the goal of improving overall public health.

**diagnosis**—to determine what is wrong with a patient. This process is especially important because it will determine the type of treatment the patient receives.

**diagnostic testing**—any tests performed to help determine a medical diagnosis.

**EKG machine**—an electrocardiogram (EKG or ECG) is a test that checks for problems with the electrical activity of your heart. An EKG shows the heart's electrical activity as line tracings on paper. The spikes and dips in the tracings are called waves. The heart is a muscular pump made up of four chambers.

**first responder**—the initial personnel who rush to the scene of an accident or an emergency.

**Health Insurance Portability and Accountability Act (HIPAA)**—a federal law enacted in 1996 that protects continuity of health coverage when a person changes or loses a job, that limits health-plan exclusions for preexisting medical conditions, that requires that patient medical information be kept private and secure, that standardizes electronic transactions involving health information, and that permits tax deduction of health insurance premiums by the self-employed.

**internship**—the position of a student or trainee who works in an organization, sometimes without pay, in order to gain work experience or satisfy requirements for a qualification.

**kinesiology**—the study of the principles of mechanics and anatomy in relation to human movement.

**Master of Science degree**—a Master of Science is a master's degree in the field of science awarded by universities in many countries, or a person holding such a degree.

**obesity**—a condition characterized by the excessive accumulation and storage of fat in the body.

**pediatrics**—the branch of medicine dealing with children.

**physiology**—a branch of biology that deals with the functions and activities of life or of living matter (as organs, tissues, or cells) and of the physical and chemical phenomena involved.

**Surgeon General**—the operational head of the US Public Health Department and the leading spokesperson for matters of public health.

# Further Reading

Grivett, Beth. *So You Want to Be a Physician Assistant.* Tennessee: Lighting Source, 2009.

Ohanesian, Jessi Rodriguez. *The Ultimate Guide to the Physician Assistant Profession.* New York: McGraw-Hill Educational Books, 2014.

Rodican, Andrew J. *How to Ace the Physician Assistant School Interview.* New York: AJR Associates, 2011.

Strange, Cordelia. *Physicians' Assistants & Nurses: New Opportunities in the 21st Century Health System.* Philadelphia: Mason Crest, 2010.

# Internet Resources

**http://www.bls.gov/ooh/health care/physician-assis-tants.htm#tab-1**

> The US Department of Labor's Bureau of Labor Statistics provides information about the career outlook for physician assistants.

**https://www.aapa.org**

> Website of the Academy of Physician Assistants.

**http://grad-schools.usnews.rankingsandreviews.com /best-graduate-schools/top-health-schools/physician-assistant-rankings**

> A *U.S. News & World Report* article that ranks physician assistant programs in the United States.

# Index

Numbers in **bold italic** refer to captions.

# About the Author

**Samantha Simon** has spent her career in healthcare: shadowing medical professionals, working in medical research, and as a patient liaison advocate within the industry. Her work authoring and writing about her experiences, and further studies into various aspects of the healthcare profession, has gained her unique insight into various aspects of the careers in the field of healthcare. Samantha received her Bachelor's Degree in Health Sciences Pre- Clinical Studies at the University of Central Florida. She has written and studied extensively in Neurobiology, Microbiology, Physiology, and Epidemiology, as well as worked on Medical Self-Assessment, Health Laws and Ethics, and Research Methods. She enjoys authoring and mentoring and lives in South Florida with her family and friends.